Learning Rounds with Teachers

BUILDING REFLECTIVE PRACTITIONERS

Dr. Marcy Roan

Principal PRINCIPLES

UNITED STATES OF AMERICA

Copyright © 2022 by Marcy Roan.

Copyright © 2022 by Marcy Roan.
All rights reserved. No part of this publication may be reproduced, distributed or transmitted in any form or by any means, including photocopying, recording, or other electronic or mechanical methods, without the prior written permission of the publisher, except in the case of brief quotations embodied in critical reviews and certain other noncommercial uses permitted by copyright law. For permission requests, write to the publisher, addressed "Attention: Permissions Coordinator," at the address below.

Marcy Roan, Author
roanmarcy@gmail.com
https://sites.google.com/view/leadlearners/home

Book design © 2017, BookDesignTemplates.com

Ordering Information: Special discounts are available on quantity purchases by corporations, associations, and others. For details, contact the publisher at the address above.

MARCY ROAN — First Edition
Print ISBN # 978-1-7346374-6-5
eBook ISBN # 978-1-7346374-7-2
Printed in the United States of America

Contents

Lessons from the Medical Field 7

Building a Reflective Staff: It's All About Growth 23

Designing Structures to Support Effective Learning Rounds 37

    Data Review (DR) 42

    Purposeful Planning (PP) 43

    Instructional Rounds (IR) 43

    Analysis of Student Work (ASW) 44

    Minute Clinics (MC) 45

Inside an Effective Learning Walk 49

Coming Full Circle: Follow-Up and Next Steps 59

    After the Learning Walk 65

    How the Process Works Together 74

Conclusion 77

References 91

About the Author 93

Dedication

This book is dedicated to all the teachers, coaches, support staff, administrators, and students who agreed to be vulnerable enough with their practice and their thinking to engage in the work of examining teaching and learning.

The profession continues to improve outcomes for students because of this willingness to look in the mirror of the work for the sole purpose of getting better.

*A practical guide to assist schools in developing a **transformative** learning rounds process.*

CHAPTER 1

Lessons from the Medical Field

Instructional rounds...have deliberately drawn on the medical model...because medicine has...the most powerful practice for analyzing and understanding its own work.   -City, Elmore, Fiarman, & Teitel, L (2009)

My mother was recently hospitalized for a serious illness. She was transferred from her home hospital to a larger teaching hospital in a metropolitan area. The transfer became medically necessary when the smaller, regional hospital couldn't properly diagnose her with their equipment and resources.

When she arrived at the teaching hospital, a team of medical personnel surrounded her and began gathering information that was visually available while other medical staff scoured the existing documents and information for any potential direction for her care, while still, other members of the team conducted medical tests.

Once the doctors and nurses determined how to proceed in the immediate, she was settled into a room, and we settled into uncertainty about the length of care or diagnosis. I quickly realized that the uncertainty around how long the illness was to last, or the lack of knowledge about exactly what was causing her illness and the hesitancy to take any action, was not an indication of a "wait and see" approach on the part of hospital staff. The staff was instead preparing for a learning approach to my mother's condition and subsequent care.

> *I quickly realized that the uncertainty around how long the illness was to last, or the lack of knowledge about exactly what was causing her illness and the hesitancy to take any action, was not an indication of a "wait and see" approach...*

The hospital staff quickly instituted a process of rounds where one representative from each area of specialization – neurology, infectious disease, cardiology, and every other department charged with her care, such as the nursing staff, physical therapy, occupational therapy, and speech — would all gather and discuss observations, medical interventions, and the impact of actions already taken.

As I watched this high-functioning team over the next few days, I noticed why City, Elmore, Fiarman, and Teitel (2009) encouraged the educational community to learn from this valuable practice. Before the team came into the room to talk about and observe my mother, they met outside the room, wheeling computer carts that provided in-the-moment detailed information regarding steps the previous hospital and emergency care had provided and the observations made around her condition since arriving at the teaching hospital.

As I watched this initial interaction of professionals, I noticed there was always one who would reference a running narrative of my mother's care. It was a lengthy description of her reaction to any medical intervention, if my mother was communicating with anyone, or if she has moved any part of her body in response to a direct question or interaction.

Another team member had all the test data – huge electronic charts that provided the results of blood tests, MRIs, or other evaluations. I also noticed a team member had on the screen a list of all medications and monitoring of breathing, heart rate, and oxygen levels to share with the team. This initial conversation happened outside her room.

Everyone in the circle contributed to the conversation. Once this initial conversation occurred, the team would converge in the room at the foot of her bed where they would have much of the same conversation, except they would be observing her current state while talking about the data just reviewed in the hall.

The difference between the conversations that occurred in the hall and the conversations at the foot of her bed while observing her current state was the focus on impact.

What if we used a similar approach (using data, best practices, high-leverage moves, multiple perspectives, and observation) when working towards the best outcome for students?

A test result would be reviewed followed typically by a known case study of expected results. The observation and conversation would then be followed by whether the stated results were consistent with what they were seeing. This conversation engaged everyone in the circle and often included colleagues challenging each other.

It was not uncommon for me to overhear a nurse, for example, respond when a doctor stated the impact of a particular approach, "I don't find that [response] to be typical in this case, Doctor. While in here the other day, the patient responded in this way – not the way you are describing." The doctor (or whoever was being challenged) would often respond by appreciating the challenge and the new perspective it provided to the specific care of the patient and shifting perspective, often to provide updated ideas about how to proceed based on the interaction.

Witnessing this environment of learning and growth with the expressed purpose of providing the best care for my mother and making sure that the actions taken (the medications and interventions) had the greatest positive impact provided me with so many parallels to the educational environment. What if we used a similar approach (using data, best practices, high-leverage moves, multiple perspectives, and observation) when working towards the best outcome for students? This is where learning rounds come in and what this resource is intended to promote.

Meeting the needs of students is what we do in classrooms and schools. Teachers spend an inordinate amount of time planning for the instruction that happens in their classrooms. They find resources and activities that they believe will engage their students while also having the intended learning outcome.

Support staff plan Tetris-like schedules that put them with students and in classrooms, often timed to the second, to provide exactly what their students need to close learning gaps and bring them to grade level. Amidst all the scheduling and planning, we hope that students' test scores at the end of it all reflect the hard work and attention to students' needs. When that doesn't happen, we feel frustrated, thinking perhaps the instruction didn't work. We blame the test, or we wonder if there is some underlying cause that we have yet to identify.

While these may all be normal reactions and may have some influence on results we find at the end of an instructional sequence, unit, quarter, or year, the reality is, at the end of the day, what we have the most control over are the instructional strategies we choose given our students current status and how we believe they will respond to the instruction or intervention.

The practice of learning rounds, just like the medical rounds I observed during my mother's illness, is designed to hone in on the highest leverage strategies for our specific students by examining the response or impact of instruction on students during the learning process. The practice of learning rounds gives teachers and schools a locus of control for the progress of students.

Rounds, made standard practice by the medical community, arose on the educational scene around 2009. Beginning at district levels, educators used collective knowledge and collaborative spirit to engage in examining pedagogy and practice across schools and classrooms.

...at the end of the day, what we have the most control over are the instructional strategies used...

Not long after, schools began to use the process as part of school improvement efforts. While the overarching premise is the same at both the district and school levels, I have found as a school principal, the practice at the building level presents slightly different impacts on culture, feedback, and change.

The practice of rounds at the school level holds significant promise for the development of reflective practitioners, the building of collective efficacy, and the strengthening of targeted effective instruction specific to a school population.

This is a different approach than your typical walkthrough procedures or supervision of instruction at the building level. As Elizabeth A. City states in her article "Learning from Instructional Rounds," "Rounds are an inquiry process. People doing rounds should expect to learn something themselves…. I think of this [versus walkthroughs or supervision] as the difference between looking through a window (supervision and evaluation) and holding up a mirror (rounds)."

Why Implement a Learning Rounds Approach?

What if you were the leader of a school where teachers and instructional support staff regularly engaged in conversations, investigations, and targeted problem-solving around instructional practices in each and every classroom?

What if your new teachers were provided with the opportunity to engage in meaningful on-the-job professional development that provided windows of experience and thinking of your most experienced teachers on a regular basis? What if your veteran teachers were able to use a process of learning rounds to get out of their teaching ruts or mentor other teachers through critical thinking and problem-solving around teaching and learning?

> *"I think of this (versus walkthroughs or supervision) as the difference between looking through a window (supervision and evaluation) and holding up a mirror (rounds)."* Elizabeth A City "Learning from Instructional Rounds"

I have yet to encounter a teacher who doesn't want their work with students to have some sort of influence, outcome, or impact. Influence, outcome, and impact are not either/or situations. They are a sliding scale. We all have influence, generate outcomes, and have an impact. The question involves what degree of impact we have and whether it is positive or negative.

The purpose of using a strategy like learning rounds is to acknowledge that a positive impact is the goal. Teachers and schools who build a practice of successful learning rounds ultimately result in mindsets that put impact, accountability, and a dialogue-rich environment at the center of the work. Hattie and Zierer (2018) believe there are mindsets that have an impact on student achievement, and several of them are foundationally ingrained in the work of successful learning rounds. In 10 Mindframes for Visible Learning, Hattie and Zierer describe the following mindsets, which are believed to have a significant effect on student achievement and frame the work of engaging in learning rounds:

1) My fundamental task is to evaluate the effect of my teaching on students' learning and achievement.
2) The success and failure of my student's learning are about what I do or don't do.
3) I want to talk more about learning than teaching.
4) Assessment is about my impact.

The process of learning rounds supports these mindsets – the reason we do this teaching work is to have an impact, and we examine our work to determine the level of impact. In order to have some impact, it is critical to prioritize the practice and to make sure that the practice and the time it takes to assure the process are important parts of your learning process in schools. Additionally, in Correlates of Effective Schools, Lawrence W. Lezotte identifies "...one of the characteristics of the most effective schools is their willingness to declare that some things are more important than others; they are willing to abandon some less important [tasks]...to be able to have enough time dedicated to those areas that are valued the most." (p. 4)

In order to give learning rounds this level of significance, we have to commit to the process and to the consistency of implementation. This is a huge cultural change, and the implementation hiccups we may experience along the way could serve to thwart efforts. Please don't underestimate the importance of a culture shift. The nature of culture can make or break a school and its ability to make progress. Commitment and consistency are key. Learning rounds need to be a priority. This may mean that due to having a substitute in the building, we may need to adjust a class we visit or even move a learning round to another day, but it needs to happen. As noted in Learning Rounds: What the Literature Tells Us (and What It Doesn't), Philpott, Carey, and Oates (2015), "Change, they argue, will only come about if

Instructional Rounds becomes systemic. It will not result from isolated or irregular practice of Instructional Rounds. City et al (2009) go as far as to suggest that isolated examples of Instructional Rounds will exacerbate the very problem they were developed to remedy."

The purpose of this guide is to assist school leaders and school staff charged with supporting instructional practices in a building in the development of a learning rounds process in their school. This resource is not meant to be a comprehensive guide to learning rounds, nor is it meant to provide the research base around the practice of learning rounds for educators. I suggest great resources for additional reading and learning in the resource section of the book. This resource assumes that there is a desire to start the practice and that there are some important aspects from lessons learned that may help principals build a sustainable practice of learning rounds in their buildings.

The Problem of Practice Approach

The research around the learning rounds approach often begins with the identification of a problem of practice. A problem of practice as it relates to learning rounds is essentially the identification of a focus for the learning rounds. Obviously, a good problem of practice is one that would be observable in a classroom instructional setting. A strong problem of practice is something that could be acted upon and is aligned to the broader school improvement goals.

Many learning rounds protocols list the identification of a problem of practice as something that is done as a means of identifying the focus of the round occurring before the rounds even take place. While there is power in this approach, this resource includes the use of rounds to identify the focus. In my experience in conducting learning rounds at the school level, I have found it to be productive and meaningful to review data prior to the rounds to identify where or which students are struggling and then conducting rounds with the intent to see if we can find a link from instructional practices. The value of the problem of practice is not to be understated. As stated in Stephanie McConnell's Win Time, "In essence, guiding your school to think about the challenges and problems the school is experiencing will determine the root cause of the issue, what circumstances are being determined, and the steps the school can take to make a greater impact and difference in student learning." (p. 11)

I have spent the last ten years planning and conducting learning rounds as a district coach and as a school principal. I have worked with amazing teams to build and strengthen this practice in ways that positively impact teacher efficacy and drive student achievement.

> *I never thought that making this commitment would have the long-term unintended consequences of making the work of schools easier because everyone is engaged in the problem-solving, instructional excellence, and collective accountability that comes from learning rounds.*

First, let me acknowledge as a principal that when we are given a new initiative to implement or have a great idea that we believe in passionately, it can be hard not to hit the ground running. I encourage you to ground yourself in the idea that you want to go slow to go fast. It is imperative that we spend the time and attention needed to build a learning culture supportive of not just going into each other's classrooms, but of being willing to look at the evidence objectively for the purpose of growing ourselves and our students.

As a turnaround principal, I also know what it feels like when there are so many things to focus on that trying to find time to focus on just one thing brings on a panic attack of enormous proportions. I felt this way before I worked on my campus to integrate a practice of learning rounds, and I certainly felt this way at times during the implementation of learning rounds. It is definitely a commitment for a school leader to devote so much time and energy into learning rounds when there are fires to be put out every day in a school building.

What I will tell you, though, is that I never thought that making this commitment would have the long-term unintended consequences of making the work of schools easier because everyone is engaged in the problem-solving, instructional excellence, and collective accountability that comes from learning rounds.

So, you want to begin a process of learning rounds at your school?

Awesome!

Let's get started.

CHAPTER 2

Building a Reflective Staff: It's All About Growth

Progress is impossible without change, and those who cannot change their minds cannot change anything.   -George Bernard Shaw

I have had many leader mentors through my career and contribute much of the leader I am today to these strong, compassionate, and effective leader models. Early in my coaching career, a leader mentor shared with me the importance of keeping what he referred to as leader notes. These leader notes were really nothing more than a chronical of the daily leader interactions, decisions, and outcomes. While this approach was more for capturing actions for later reference, I began using it as a means of reflection.

At the end of the day, I could look over the decisions I made and the impact or outcome and reflect on whether the result was aligned to my goal or intentions. This rudimentary practice was the beginning of my focus on reflection and the profound influence it had over desired results. I believe that a strong practice in reflection is key for educators to track our educational decisions. Just like the physician trying to cure a patient, they reflect on actions and observe the resulting outcome of each medical step to confirm that the next decision is based on these lessons learned from previous decisions.

Learning from a reflection of our decisions and actions is how **GROWTH** happens. We are going to use GROWTH as an acronym for the steps of the learning rounds process where each letter refers to an action or a focus. A description of each letter is included below and will be referenced again as we move through the process to show where each step fits.

G**row Culture.** This is a critical step in the success of your learning rounds process. Failure to take time to establish a culture that is supportive of this extremely vulnerable process can do more harm in the long run as teachers may become critical of the process and see it more as a "gotcha" experience.

Reflect on Available Data. Another essential first step is to examine all available data to generate some potential areas of focus for learning rounds. This includes numeric and anecdotal/walkthrough data.

Observe Students and Task First. During the learning rounds process, we want to zero in on the task that students are working on. When students are provided with grade-level rigorous tasks, we are in a better position to accurately determine potential impact of instruction. Pay attention to what students are asked to do and how they are responding to what they are asked to do. Are they disengaged, confused, done quickly?

Watch for Evidence of Impact. While all these elements contribute to building a reflective practice of learning rounds, the evidence of impact is really where the rubber meets the road. This is the distinction between teaching and learning.

Talk about Actions and Evidence. If the time we are in the classroom during learning rounds is about collecting evidence of impact, then the follow-up conversations about what we notice are equally important to building collective capacity and calibrating what we see.

Highlight High-Leverage Action. With so many minute-by-minute decisions that happen in a classroom during the day, and with no shortage of options for teachers to use when it comes to instruction and tasks, it is crucial that we identify the actions and tasks through this process that produce the greatest impact for students.

Focusing on these elements of the learning rounds process helps to build these strong reflective practices, which can be the difference between sustainable success and pockets of success across a building. It's likely you have reflective teachers in your building right now. It's most often those teachers who have it. You know what I mean – those teachers that get consistent results from their students, often have multiple tracking and organization strategies for knowing where kids are in their learning, and their classroom often runs like a well-oiled machine. While other teachers may learn to mimic the observable traits, such as spreadsheets and management, results may often elude them.

So, what is it and how can we support all teachers in developing it? In my experience as a coach and a school administrator, it is the reflective practice effective teachers insist upon and take time to do that results in consistent progress from students. Our job as school administrators is to promote and build the capacity of reflection in our staff. Before we begin talking about building reflection in staff, it's important for you to start with your own reflection. Just as you would with any other large initiative or new process you would implement in your building, you must have a vision for the work. Vision supports clarity and provides a common WHY to the work we are getting ready to put our time, effort, and attention on.

Before you start initiating the learning rounds process with your staff, it is important for you, as the school leader, to spend some time thinking about two things.

1) Why is this important to do right now?

2) What will the ideal learning rounds process look and feel like when it is up and running as a sustainable function of my school?

Please don't underestimate the power of these two reflective questions. Building a sustainable learning rounds process in your building requires all staff buy-in and belief in the power of the practice.

As a leader, you would reflect on these two questions first. This helps you gain clarity of vision that will support the process moving forward. These questions also assume your desire to build buy-in through your staff. In addition, due to the learning rounds process being a whole school effort, you are going to need as much of your staff on board as possible to support sustainability.

Our job as school administrators is to promote and build the capacity of reflection in our staff.

After you have done this reflection for yourself, you will want to begin involving your staff in the similar learning and reflective process. You'll find a template for this process in the resource section of this book. (Resource 1)

The next step you'll need to take involves a team structure for rounds. While schools have a different language, or terms, to describe the teams they have, many have a team structure whose work is to provide guidance and be a voice for a representative group in the building. This structure is often referred to as a school improvement team. If this is the only widely represented team structure you have, then you can begin this work through that team. Other effective structures that would be ideal to take on this work are instructional and multi-tiered student support (MTSS) teams.

Once you have determined which team structure you will be using to begin learning rounds work in your building, it's time to start building the foundation that will serve as the common language and calibration for the group when it comes time to examine the data from the rounds. I urge you not to rush or eliminate this step! You are embarking on a practice that can be interpreted as evaluative, punitive, or downright stressful for educators, even if you already have a consistent, frequent walkthrough practice in place.

The primary purpose of learning rounds is not to provide feedback for the teacher, but to engage the learning rounds group in the examination of teaching and learning.

Why? Because this process is not about the teacher. If you have a walkthrough process in place, the main purpose is to provide feedback for the teacher based on your observation. The primary purpose of learning rounds is not to provide feedback for the teacher, but to engage the learning rounds group in the examination of teaching and learning. This will be a shift for many teachers. They will worry about what the group saw and even, in the case of an already reflective teacher, beg for some feedback. You must spend the time building a knowledge base and creating a culture that will support this very different approach.

Once you have designated the team you will use to initially engage in this work, you want to spend time reading about learning rounds and discussing your intent and vision for the process.

I have done this a few different ways, but I always begin with research and reading. I share articles prior to a meeting that I ask the team to read so we can spend the time during our meeting discussing what was read. Sometimes I provide guiding questions such as, "What do you see as a benefit for us to try something like this? What comes up for you as a concern as you read this?" If I provide questions, they are often basic in nature and provide a way for participants to feel comfortable examining the idea in the group. I want to have an honest discussion around the topic and provide both pro/con questions so that no one feels like the "negative voice" at the table. I ask them all to consider both sides.

Here are a few resources I have used to support building the collective understanding of learning rounds in education:

1. "Learning from Instructional Rounds" by Elizabeth City
2. Improving Teaching and Learning through Instructional Rounds by Lee Tietel
3. Creating a Cycle of Continuous Learning through Instructional Rounds by Catherine L. Meyer-Looze
4. Making the Most of Instructional Rounds by Robert Marzano

These critical first steps in learning about the purpose of learning rounds, becoming clear about your why, and building the base for the practice in your school support a strong foundation for the work and are the basis for the first component of **GROWTH-G for Grow Culture.**

Grow Culture. This is a critical step in the success of your learning rounds process. Failure to take time to establish a culture that is supportive of this extremely vulnerable process can do more harm in the long run as teachers may become critical of the process and see it more as a "gotcha" experience.

Remember, opening classrooms as learning labs for a school is a level of vulnerability for the observer and the observed that may be new for many staff. Take the time to evaluate your staff's comfort level with an understanding of the purpose and process for learning rounds.

> Fisher and Frey (2014) also discuss the importance of building culture in their article "Using Teacher Learning Walks to Improve Instruction": "Issues of trust must be dealt with directly, and professional development and discussion should precede practice. The investment in time

> and conversation is well worth the effort so that learning walks are viewed positively from their inception."

A close second to building the culture of reflection is making sure that we know the baseline for where we begin. This means spending time going over data. This could be both formative and summative assessment data, informal data, and anecdotal data such as the information you gather when you conduct classroom walkthroughs. The focus organizer (Resource 1) can be used as a tool for you to collect multiple forms of information so that you can begin to look for trends in what you see. This information can provide the focus for your learning walks. The examination of data is reflected in the second letter of our acronym GROWTH. The **Reflect on Available Data** reminds us to take the time to reflect on what is currently happening in our buildings.

Reflect on Available Data. Another essential first step is to examine all available data to generate some potential areas of focus for learning rounds. This includes numeric and anecdotal/walkthrough data.

Data permeates the educational landscape, so this seems like a no-brainer. The reminder is more about making sure that we are gathering and examining all available data — quantitative and qualitative. Collecting assessment data, MTSS data, observation data, and professional learning community notes that reference successes and challenges can be great windows into a focus for learning walks with teachers. Not only can you use this data to determine the focus of your learning walks, but gathering this information can also be helpful for identifying trends of practices that you want to continue schoolwide. I found this particularly useful when we were reopening during the pandemic as I wanted to highlight those things teachers were doing that were making a difference for our students.

We need to begin by clearly defining our starting point. ***Resource 1*** can help you begin to gather this information. We need to make sure we are collecting not just the quantifiable data, but the anecdotal as well. The Focus Organizer helps you identify noticeable patterns that already exist as evidenced by all the information you have on hand. You may have all this information already collected and in separate documents in files, on walls, or on websites. I encourage you to gather this information on one page. With data divided across many areas, it can be harder to get the overview that we want to begin this process. Gathering this information gives us the big picture overview that provides context for where we are as a school before beginning this process. If you will use the learning rounds process to develop a problem of practice, it is also helpful to spend time thinking about what your expectations are around teaching and learning.

For example, if you expect staff to develop instruction that is grounded in a problem-based learning approach, then it is important to determine what that looks like in a classroom and what you might expect to see if you were to walk into a classroom that is fully immersed in a problem-based learning approach.

As leaders, we may identify these kinds of practices and believe they are important enough to establish them as schoolwide expectations. This process can be instrumental in solidifying those practices you have determined to be the basis of your school's teaching and learning approach. You may not have any identified schoolwide approach like problem-based learning, but you may have expectations such as posting a learning standard, an essential question, or an agenda. This information is also part of your data-gathering approach.

Once you have spent time reflecting, building a culture that will support the process of learning rounds, and collecting the available qualitative and quantitative data, it's time to look at structures for the rounds process.

CHAPTER 3

Designing Structures to Support Effective Learning Rounds

Change will not come if we wait for some other person or some other time. We are the ones we've been waiting for. We are the change that we seek.
– Barak Obama

So, let's talk nuts and bolts. The organization of learning rounds can sometimes feel like herding cats, but if we continually go back to the why of this work, the focus on organizing the rounds is worth the time. First, we need to determine the purpose of the upcoming round. This is where your data review, information gathered around teaching and learning, school improvement team, or your instructional team meeting information can be mined for a focus.

Before we get detailed about the learning rounds themselves, let's look at the big picture of teams in the building and how they factor into the learning rounds process. I started the learning rounds process with my teams. First, I created an instructional team. This is not the team that gets together to discuss school improvement strategies. This is a team designed to investigate and learn from the current practices occurring in the building.

The instructional team is the auditing body that examines how our goals, strategies, and impact are showing up in our daily practices. The team included my administration, my instructional coaches, and a representative from each content/grade level. Depending on the size of your school, you may use folks from your school improvement team. The number of teams and the name of teams is not the point. The point is that we have a group of educators who represent each area of our building that spend time examining the impact of teaching in our building.

If you are in a small building, having a designated instructional team may not be workable. That's ok. You could use an already existing structure such as your improvement team to do this work as well. The point is that you have a team that has dedicated time to examine how the instructional goals of the building are showing up in everyday practice.

Once my instructional team was developed, my professional learning communities (PLCs) were structured. You may already have a professional learning community structure or a standard agenda that teachers follow when they are conducting these meetings. While this was also true for me, I had one meeting a week that was facilitated by my instructional coaches and administration. It was this one meeting that I used to rotate the following activities: data analysis, instructional planning, learning walks, and analysis of student work. Prior to the beginning of the year, administration and instructional coaching staff would map out these four tasks for the entire year so we could be purposeful in our conversations and work. For example, we would map out our standard test measures and pair the data results dates with the data analysis professional learning community meetings. This PLC calendar was shared with staff at the beginning of the year.

Once I have these two teams assigned, there is a specific working relationship between them. The instructional team meets once a month. This team is responsible for supporting and informing the teacher learning walks – to compile the information gathered from the professional learning community (PLC) data analysis and our school improvement team. These meetings begin with reviewing the data summaries from the PLC data analysis sessions so that the team can see how each PLC group is impacting student progress. We also review general observations from walkthroughs. This information and the discussion that ensues sets the stage for the gathering of insight through learning walks. Of course, at the beginning of the year, the learning walks that the instructional team conducts are to "see what we see" based on our communicated expectations, vision, and school improvement actions. I believe the most important aspect of successful learning walks to building reflective practice with teachers is to be consistent. Like many things in our buildings that threaten to hijack the meetings, professional learning, or other activities that may seem "optional," or what may be the first to go when all those "have to" items push our schedules around, learning rounds fall under what many see as moveable when people and meetings demand our attention.

In order for learning rounds to have the intended results and develop a strong culture of reflective practice and improvement, they must be prioritized and protected. I have read, although I don't recall the source, that what sets apart principals who are successful in turning around schools is their relentless focus on what matters. If you are implementing learning rounds because you believe in the power of building teacher-reflective practice to transform schools, then a commitment to making sure the learning rounds happen needs to be your priority.

Let's take a minute to discuss PLCs specifically. There is plenty of research on the importance and purpose of consistent PLCs, and I don't intend to revisit that body of work here. I do want to highlight the connection between PLCs and the rounds process. Many researchers indicate that PLCs need to result in a contribution to collective knowledge, not just individual knowledge (Stoll et al, 2006). This is at the very heart of the learning rounds process. The learning together that is immersed in the work contributes to this collective knowledge and provides extensive relevance. Let's face it – when we are in a planning PLC, we use the knowledge of where students are and what they need, but at the end of the day, this is still hypothetical until we are able to see how the planning pans out with students.

There are similarities between the focus and purpose of PLCs and the process and purpose of learning rounds. Here are some ideas the two processes have in common:

1. They are both centered on student learning (outcome and impact).
2. Both processes are meant to promote systemic collaboration and a focus on group versus individual learning.
3. PLCs and learning rounds seek to promote a shared culture and knowledge.
4. Both of these experiences use, analyze, and generate data around learning.

At this point, if you have already established a rotation for your rounds, then those dates can be planned out at any point. I used a four-focus rotation for my administrative facilitated PLCs. The fifth focus was added as a result of supporting schools with a need to maximize professional development times and to support new teachers more. Each of the areas of focus are defined as follows:

Data Review (DR)

Data Review (DR): Data Review PLCs is a dedicated time for us to examine all the information that we are gathering about student performance: standard assessments, common assessments, progress monitoring, and exit slips. With the increase of data from so many sources, an organization of data analysis may include separate meetings for each source. For example, one could include core data, supplemental data reviews, and reviews for those students receiving the most intensive support or in review for the potential of increasing the level of support.

Purposeful Planning (PP)

Purposeful Planning (PP): This PLC is for planning with teachers around the data we are collecting. Teachers come to the planning session with their students initially grouped and with some ideas of what they plan to do to address concerns. The time we spend in this planning is really trying to make sure that we have clearly identified the gap and have the strongest strategies we can in place for the reteach.

Instructional Rounds (IR)

Instructional Rounds (IR): This is where we conduct our rounds and gather information (like the process described in this text).

If we have identified a concern from the planning PLC or from our own observations/walkthroughs, we can examine it further.

Analysis of Student Work (ASW)

Analysis of Student Work (ASW): This part of our process is deeply integrated with the other aspects of the PLCs. We have analyzed student work as a part of the data PLC and the planning PLC, and we have analyzed student work as a part of instructional rounds. The ASW typically consists of teachers coming to the PLC with student work from a common assessment. Part of the pre-work can also include a teacher's reflection of what the work would look like if the standard was met. This development of an exemplar is an important part of backwards planning and can also be completed as part of the planning process on the front end. If the common assessment is a part of an instructional sequence, a student exemplar from the complete standard may not be applicable to the analysis of the student work. Once teachers have assembled the work and have grouped students according to demonstrated needs, the teachers create a plan for whole and small-group focus and instructional strategies that may be used.

Minute Clinics (MC)

Minute Clinics (MC): Minute clinics are an addition to my traditional PLC rotation. Minute clinics are a PLC designed to provide quick professional development and opportunity to practice strategies or skills that could improve instruction. For example, if we noticed in rounds that engagement improved when teachers asked high-quality, in-depth questions, the following PLC Minute Clinic would focus on how to write, deliver, and plan for high-quality, in-depth questions.

Below is an example of a schedule layout of PLC meetings that are mapped out at the beginning of the year. The benefit of mapping out these meetings is the accountability that is inherent for planning them out. Once all the meetings are on the calendar for the entire year, there is resistance in canceling them, and it is less likely that folks will have other reasons why they can't attend. It also allows for purposely mapping them against other school or district happenings, like assessments.

I typically start with mapping the data PLC based on when our standardized assessments occur and then plug in the other PLC topics around that.

Weekly PLCs								
Sept 6	DR	Nov 7	MC	Jan 30	ASW	April 3	LR
Sept 12	PP	Nov 14	DR	Feb 6	MC	April 17	ASW
Sept 19	LR	Nov 21	PP	Feb 13	DR	April 24	MC
Sept 26	ASW	Nov 28	LR	Feb 21	PP	May 1	DR
Oct 3	MC	Dec 5	ASW	Feb 27	LR	May 8	PP
Oct 10	DR	Dec 12	MC	March 6	ASW	May 15	LR
Oct 17	PP	Jan 9	DR	March 13	MC	May 22	ASW
Oct 24	LR	Jan 17	PP	March 20	DR	May 30	MC
Nov 1	ASW	Jan 23	LR	March 27	PP	June 5	DR

Once this map is created, it is a shared document for all involved. Creating a PLC structure that supports this process is an important step in creating a system that integrates with other teams and systems you may already have in your building. It is not enough to create the schedule, though. We need to make this a priority. The planning time of teachers is too often the first to sacrifice when we have other, immediate concerns that need to be addressed.

Exceptional school leaders succeed because of how they use their time. These leaders recognize the importance of developing the practice and impact of teaching on learning. Because we work with humans, the learning landscape is frequently changing. Just think of the last two years, for example. The challenges students bring to the school building are significantly impacted by the disruption of a global pandemic. If we return to teaching as we have always done simply because students are back in the building for face-to-face learning, then we are ignoring the impact of the last several years and how that impact altered not just what teaching we were able to do but the very brain chemistry of the learner.

CHAPTER 4

Inside an Effective Learning Walk

Investment in infrastructure is a long-term requirement for growth and a long-term factor that will make growth sustainable. – Chando Kochhar, CEO of ICICI Bank

Let's take a look into the process of learning rounds. To begin, there is no one right way to conduct learning rounds. Because I use learning rounds for school transformation, I typically begin the rounds process by making the first round an information-gathering walk. This speaks to the building of culture from an earlier chapter. The first round is a low-stakes visit where I want participants to focus attention on what the teacher is doing/saying and what the students are doing/saying. During this first round, I also make sure that there is a thank-you left for the teachers we visit. Since we are not providing feedback to the teacher in each classroom we visit, I leave a small token of appreciation for opening up their classroom to this kind of visit.

While there is no one way to schedule a learning round, there are some standard planning steps. In general, planning a round consists of the following action steps:

- Build a schedule of 10- to 15-minute classroom visits. For the first few rounds, this may be determined by best schedule or where there are no substitutes for the day. Once you get the rounds process underway and begin to identify potential problems of practice, you may be more intentional to select a few classrooms where you expect to see either a problem of practice successfully demonstrated or a classroom you identify as strong and perhaps a few where you may be unsure or know there is work to be done.

- Each participant in the rounds process will need some basic materials, particularly if they are new to your building, haven't ventured into other classrooms or areas before, or you have a large group that you want to break up to no more than three in a classroom at a time. Remember, even teachers that are in your same building may not know exactly where to find particular teachers, as most teachers may gather in the lounge or common area versus seeking colleagues out in individual classrooms. Consider providing the following materials for each participant: a rounds schedule that includes the teacher, visit time (start and end), items to record notes (clipboard, paper, notepad, sticky notes, pens), a school map with classroom locations marked/highlighted, and the location of a secure meeting place for follow-up discussion.

- Prep staff for the rounds, assuring they understand the walk-through is not about the individual teacher but about the evidence. (No individual feedback is provided to the observed teacher.)
- Optional: Select a thank-you to leave in each observed classroom.

In a previous chapter, I talked about the two team structures that regularly engage in this work: the instructional team and PLCs. I always began with the instructional team for learning rounds. I used this group walk to be more information-gathering. I did this so that I could use the initial PLC teacher rounds to build the culture of the rounds process. So, during one teacher meeting a month, teachers engage in learning rounds (see the PLC planning chart in Chapter 3) . The first learning round is for getting used to the process and looking at classrooms with the intention of learning and reflection. For this round, the primary goal is to have teachers take note of the task students are asked to do and how students are responding to the task. This is the essence of the **O for Observe Students and Task First** and the **W for Watch for Evidence of Impact** in the GROWTH acronym.

Observe Students and Task First. During the learning rounds process, we want to zero in on the task that students are working on. When students are provided with grade-level rigorous tasks, we are in a better position to accurately determine potential impact of instruction. Pay attention to what students are asked to do and how they are responding to what they are asked to do. Are they disengaged, confused, done quickly?

It is also important to identify the intended grade-level standard the teacher has indicated. Some states have content standards apps that you can download to your phone or tablet.

When you focus on observing how students are responding to instruction, you are working the educational muscle of identifying evidence of impact.

In order for learning walks to have the intended results and develop a strong culture of reflective practices and improvement, they must be prioritized and protected.

Because there is no shortage of what we could provide for students to do (the task) for any given instructional focus, master teaching becomes about selecting the instructional task that provides the biggest bang for the learning buck when taking into account the student readiness, skill, and instructional sequence.

The second focus we have when in learning rounds is to watch for the evidence of impact. Impact is the purpose of the entire process. Let's pause here at impact for a moment. Online dictionaries define impact as the affect or influence on something. I would also suggest we include effect or a change, which is the result or consequence of something in our definition of impact. In the conversation of teaching and learning, we are indeed talking about influencing with our teaching to the extent that we see change as a result or consequence of the decisions we make when teaching. You may also want to consider the word evidence. What constitutes evidence of learning? The student work is the evidence of learning. Student work takes the form of an assignment on a piece of paper, writing that explains thinking, the building or constructing of a tangible outcome, or the discussion students have during the course of instruction. The terms evidence and impact are the cornerstone of the **W** in the **GROWTH** acronym.

Watch for Evidence of Impact. While all these elements contribute to building a reflective practice of learning rounds, the evidence of impact is really where the rubber meets the road. This is the distinction between teaching and learning.

While this sounds simplistic, it's not. The purpose of learning rounds is to build reflective practice around teaching and learning. It is for this purpose that we don't want to just wander into a teacher's classroom and have observers just take notes of what they see. It would not serve the purpose well if we took that approach and observers left with ideas around room arrangement, bulletin board design, or cute worksheets that could not be tied to the impact of adult action on student learning (impact).

Let's take a minute to define learning. Learning is "a process that leads to change, which occurs as a result of experience and increases the potential for improved performance and future learning" (Ambrose et al, 2010, p. 3). The purpose of learning rounds is to identify the actions of adults that result in learning, particularly in a positive direction. Impact is a generic term. It can be positive, negative, or neutral. So, in the context of learning rounds, impact can positively impact learning, meaning students learned more as a result of the adult actions. Impact is negative when the ability to correlate actions to outcomes is unclear or there is confusion as to the intended outcome. Neutral impact means there is no change in the learning after the adult interaction.

While identifying impact is our ultimate goal, we do need to start building reflective muscle. For the initial learning rounds, I have a very simple note-taking form that focuses the observer on the actions of the teacher and the actions of the students. You can find the reproducible note catchers and a planning document in **RESOURCES 2-6**.

I have also simply folded a page vertically in my notebook with one side for what the teacher is doing and the other for what students are doing. This very basic beginning with open-ended noticings is the foundation of building reflective practices with teachers. These initial learning walks are simple and just serve to have participants begin with learning how to focus observation on what will soon become evidence for impact.

Another approach is to use sticky notes where teachers write their observations on a singular sticky note. This approach helps to be able to organize and categorize thoughts later into problems of practice or common trends in teaching and learning.

The organization of learning rounds predominantly circles around time and availability. With all the busyness that happens during the day in a building, someone is always in the lunchroom, on the playground, or in elective classes. The power of learning rounds, particularly when you can visit any classroom in your building, can be capitalized on if you have identified through your instructional or school improvement teams an area of building focus. For example, if it's been noted in my school improvement plan that we are focusing on higher-level questions to improve critical thinking skills, any class and any subject could be the focus of learning rounds. If we are focusing on a skill or strategy that is content-area specific, our ability to use learning rounds as a whole school to further that work may be more challenging depending on the master schedule. It doesn't make it less important. It simply means it may be more challenging to make the learning rounds more targeted for school improvement.

I have conducted rounds both ways, with a predetermined focus that has stemmed out of what our data suggested, goals from our school improvement plan, a new curriculum implementation, or perhaps a high number of first-year or beginning teachers. There is no one best way to conduct rounds; it really depends on you and your school situation. I have also used the first few rounds to build the confidence and capacity of those conducting rounds and to calibrate everyone by looking for something specific. For example, if you have identified that a strong start to class is a necessary implementation and expectation for your school this year, you may have your first set of rounds occur at the beginning of a class period and take note of the impact (positive, negative, or neutral) of the beginning of class routines you find occurring.

Regardless of the focus and classroom you identify for learning rounds at the beginning, the important thing is to begin the process. Identify it as a priority, put systems in place for it to occur on a regular basis, and spend time talking about the outcome of each round.

CHAPTER 5

Coming Full Circle: Follow-Up and Next Steps

...those who can't...don't know they can't. According to what's now known as the Dunning-Kruger effect, it's when we lack competence that we're most likely to be brimming with overconfidence. – Adam M. Grant, <u>Think Again: The Power of Knowing What You Don't Know</u>

Coming full circle may suggest that most of the hard work has already been completed, but actually, after those engaged with learning rounds and this reflective process can attest, once you learn what you don't know and what you may have to do in order to improve outcomes and increase instructional impact, the hardest part can be deciding what to do next and doing what it takes to make the change stick.

This is often the most challenging part of the whole process — how do you create this system so that it serves as a vehicle for school transformation and doesn't just get lost in the hustle and bustle of school and all the other things that demand our attention? While the names of your committees and processes may vary, I have included a description of how I implemented learning walks as an integral part of my school transformation. This is where the last two elements of GROWTH come in, talking about actions and evidence, and highlighting high-leverage action.

Let's start with the discussion about action and evidence. As stated earlier in the text, we want to build capacity and reflective practice. The way we measure our capacity progress is through the evidence shown by students. This next focus derives from the reflection and discussion around the action and evidence provided by the learning rounds observations. This step is reflected in the **T** of the **GROWTH** acronym.

T‍**alk about Actions and Evidence.** If the time we are in classrooms during learning rounds is about collecting evidence of impact, then the follow-up conversations about what we notice are equally important to building collective capacity and calibrating what we see.

The focus of the walks is geared around actions and evidence, as that is where the IMPACT can be found. The discussion of evidence is an objective process where we are looking for and lifting up the patterns of evidence we see in our visits. I will briefly describe the two-step process I have used for organizing the evidence we observe. Then we will move to the discussion and process that occurs after the learning round.

1. **Individually.** Participants of the rounds examine the notes they have made and identify 2-3 key noticings that were made during the observations. Essentially, what are the 2-3 things that you consider the most significant pieces of evidence?

2. **Pattern Seeking.** Once individuals have identified 2-3 significant observations, the group spends time reading and sorting the sticky notes, looking for patterns.

The following pictures are examples of this process. The smaller sticky notes are what individual teachers observed, and the "title" above is the pattern that the evidence revealed.

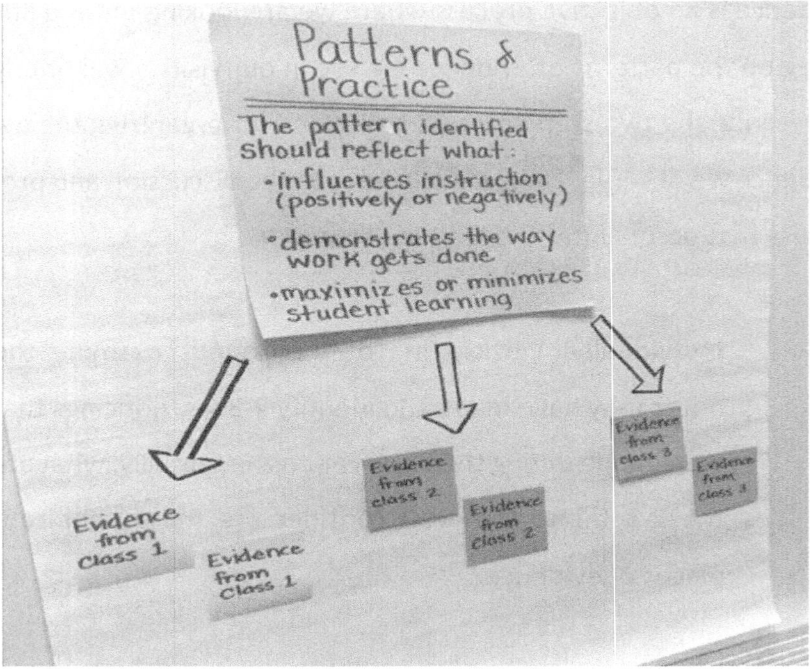
Patterns &
Practice
The pattern identified
should reflect what:
• influences instruction
(positively or negatively)
• demonstrates the way
work gets done
• maximizes or minimizes
student learning
Evidence from Class 1
Evidence from Class 1
Evidence from class 2
Evidence from class 2
Evidence from class 3
Evidence from class 3

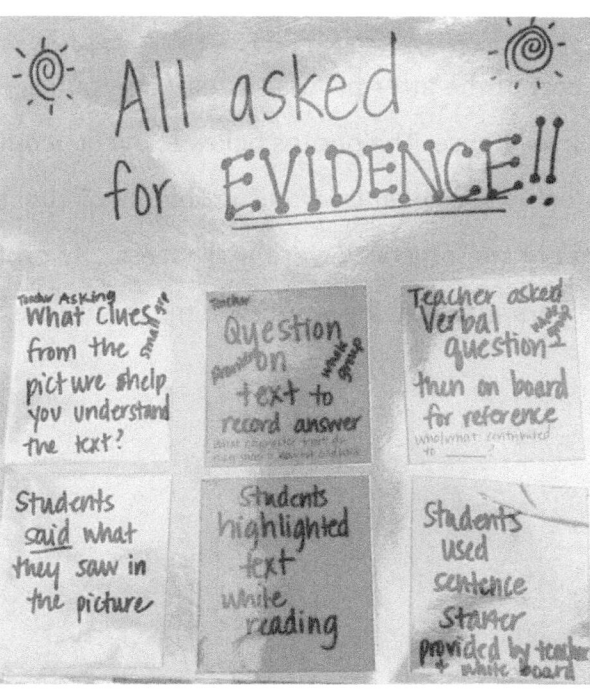

All asked for EVIDENCE!!

Teacher Asking "What clues from the picture help you understand the text?"	Teacher Question on text to record answer	Teacher asked Verbal question then on board for reference
Students *said* what they saw in the picture	Students highlighted text while reading	Students used sentence starter provided by teacher + white board

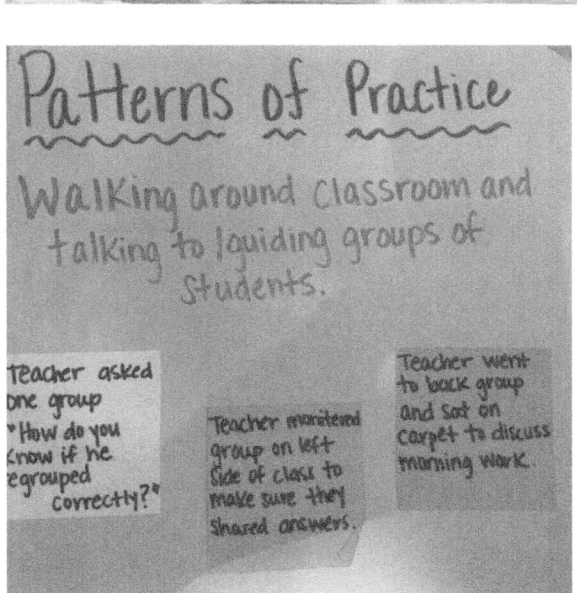

Patterns of Practice

Walking around classroom and talking to /guiding groups of students.

Teacher asked one group "How do you know if he regrouped correctly?"	Teacher monitored group on left side of class to make sure they shared answers.	Teacher went to back group and sat on carpet to discuss morning work.

As part of the after-process in learning rounds, we discuss patterns in evidence. The photos below show how our collective observations were organized and problems of practice identified. Some of the practices were not necessarily problems, but rather celebrations that we wanted to make sure we continued.

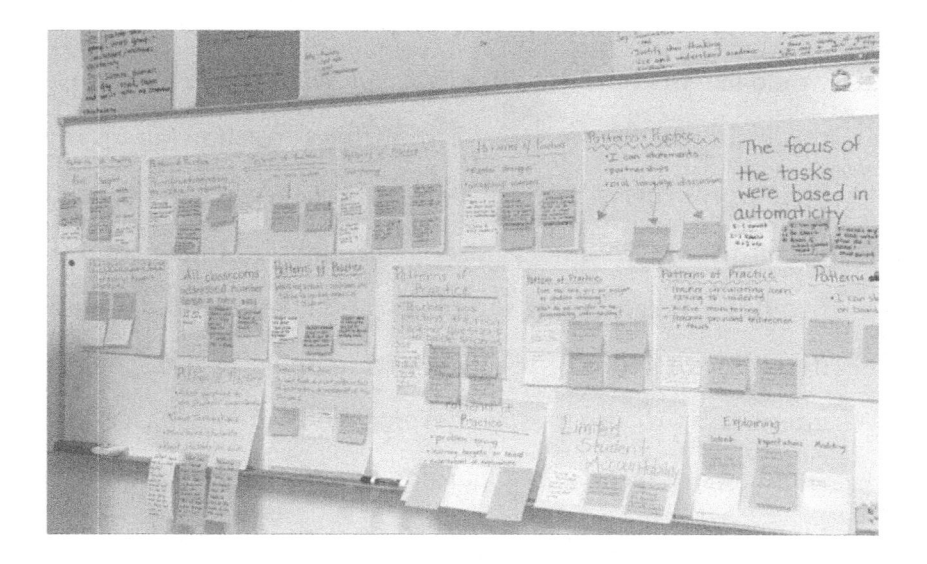

After the Learning Walk

Without impact, innovation is just an idea with a promise. — Judith Rodin, Philanthropist

So after the learning walks occur and participants have generated a pattern of practice based on their notes, these patterns either become practices we want to keep (like the previous picture where all asked for evidence) or we find practices that we would like to improve. Either way, we want to see how these (in this example) teacher-specific noticings are showing up in student work. This is the translation of teacher actions to student performance. "In a post-observation debrief, they use descriptive notes taken during the observations to build up a detailed descriptive picture of teaching and learning in the school. The intention is to use this to develop an evidence-based understanding of teaching and learning practice in the school. This is then used to plan what needs to be done next to develop that practice."

If you have spent time in your building developing data-driven instructional practices, you may already have a process for analyzing student work. If so, the same process can be used as a follow-up to the learning rounds you conduct. In the PLC structure outlined in Chapter 3, the analysis of student work followed the learning rounds. In the next professional learning community we convene after the learning rounds, teachers bring examples of student work to discuss. Ideally, the work is connected to the learning that was observed during the learning rounds.

To be real, this is not always possible, particularly if learning rounds and the next PLC occur too far apart, which can happen when things like holidays and testing occur between the two. I have found over the years that preparation helps to make the most of the time we need to analyze student work and to determine the next steps; it also serves to have teachers reflect on the purpose of the work, the standard addressed, and the expected outcome. See Resource 7 for a pre-student analysis worksheet.

We begin student analysis work meetings by having teachers sort the work they brought into three categories: Got It, Almost Got It, and Not Yet. We then talk about the characteristics that were used to determine which pile each student's work was placed in. Teachers also begin reflecting on what the work is demonstrating. See the pictures on the following pages where teacher notes about student performance are shown. Resources 4-6 are possible reflection sheets that can be used for teacher notes.

We haven't brought out the patterns from the walk yet; for now, we are simply calibrating ourselves to what we see and how that translates to evidence of the standard. To be honest, at first this process may highlight a need to work on aligning tasks to standards. If that is true, then our next professional learning community meeting (or several) are centered around the deconstruction of standards and what that looks like in student tasks.

Let's assume for explanation's sake that the work is aligned with the standard. We have sorted the assignments and discussed what elements are essential for each of the three stacks. This is where we bring out the evidence from learning walks and tie it into the work and results of students. If we noticed in our rounds that teachers asked students for evidence of their thinking throughout the observed time, then we would be looking for and discussing evidence in the student work, e.g., did the stack of papers where students "got it" included evidence of students thinking? If the observed learning round noted asking for evidence, how did that translate to student work? Was there evidence of students detailing their thinking in the work? If the work of students did not show students understanding and application describing evidence of their thinking, how can we modify our instruction to support more transfer?

Do we ask for evidence during teacher-directed instruction and model more specifically with sentence starters, for example, of how to think about the evidence we use to support thinking? Depending on how frequently the pattern of asking for evidence was during our walk (was it noted in only a grade level/content area, or was it noted across the building) and how frequently the ability to use evidence to support thinking was shown in student work, this may be a practice we take back to the instructional team to determine if there is additional training/support needed or if we want to elevate this practice to the whole school level and define the practice. Do we want to include a section in the lesson planning where teachers note how they will be supporting students in the gathering and documenting of evidence of their thinking?

This next picture shows an example of our student work analysis notes. For this PLC, teachers bring the work and they discuss the task and really spend time discussing the thinking required of the task. They start by thinking individually about the task (as indicated by the small sticky notes) and then generate some common themes that are captured in the larger chart.

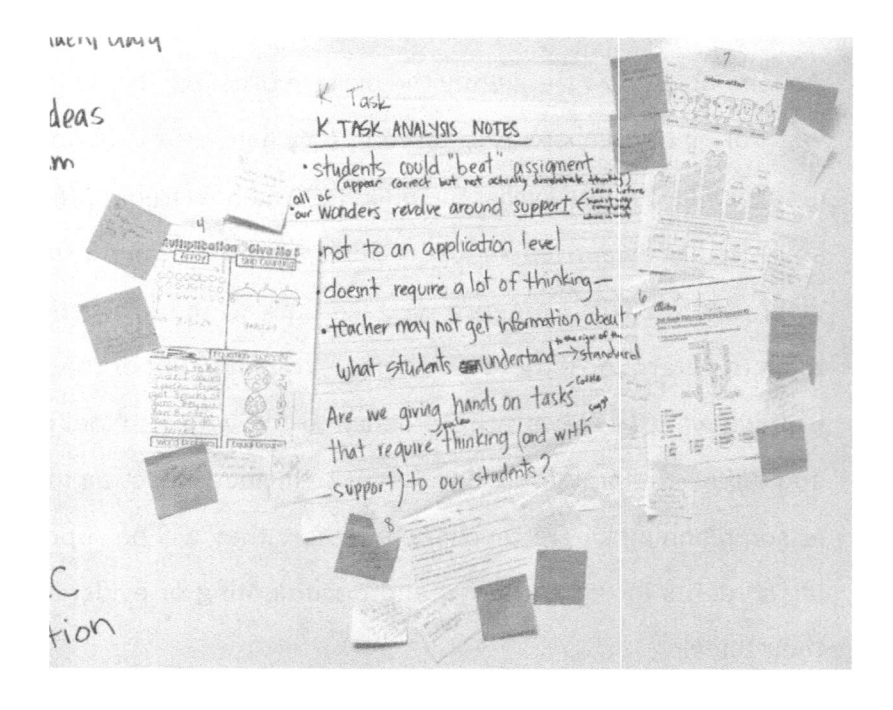

The picture below is a more individual reflection on student work that is completed by each teacher during the process of student work analysis. These two approaches show how the process could be scaffolded if the analysis of student work is a new process you are working to incorporate into your PLC practices. While it may sound like the analysis of student work is a separate process from the learning rounds, it's not. Even if it occurs as another scheduled PLC meeting, each of these processes is an integrated practice that informs and strengthens the others - all for the purpose of building reflective practice, strengthening collective efficacy, and providing deep and rigorous work for students.

> - Teacher Name Marhatta   Week of 4/20 - 4/24
> - Standard 1.0A.8 Missing # in equations
> - What was the intended outcome for the work?
>   Can students correctly solve missing number problems. This will be important for our next unit of missing # word problems.
> - How does the work demonstrate understanding of the standard?   Absent: London
>   - Example of student who understands: (0-1 wrong)
>   (5) Sammy, Greily, Carson, Kaylee, Garrett
>   - Example of student who is almost there: (2-3 wrong)
>   (8) Jamal, Anushka, Jaxson, Jayden, Adrian, Kaylen, Xavion, Gillian
>   - Example of student who does not yet understand: (4 or more)
>   (8) Uri, Honesti, Bennett, Mariah, DaVinci, Brooklyn, Zoey, Jonah
> - What's next? What will you keep doing as a result of this evidence? What will you change?
>
> | Understands | Almost | Not Yet |
> |---|---|---|
> | They will be ready to begin solving missing # word problems. Tom had some books. He gave 3 away and now has 6 left. How many are there to start? ⓢ 3 = ? ⓢ-3 = ? | They will cont. to work on missing # in small groups and will label parts. EX: __ -3 = 5   W P P ·call "parts only = add + these students are ready for WP this! | These students will have small guided math groups on missing # students with: ① label the parts ② use mini anchor chart to find rule ③ solve |

+ these students with work on +

In my support of principals with this process, I often get asked at this point, "But what if there is no pattern identified?" That's ok. Perhaps the lack of a pattern in and of itself is a pattern. Remember the purpose of the process is to build a practice of reflection.

Once the work has been done to organize and identify patterns, then we begin to discuss the high-leverage action that may need to occur. This step is reflected in the last letter of our **GROWTH** acronym, **H**. This is where we begin to examine the observations and identify potential high-leverage actions to continue or discontinue.

Highlight High-Leverage Action. With so many minute-by-minute decisions that happen in a classroom during the day, and with no shortage of options for teachers to use when it comes to instruction and task, it is crucial that we identify the actions and tasks through this process that produce the greatest impact for students.

This may take some research of high-quality sources to identify what those high-level strategies may be. For example, if I have a building of predominantly inexperienced staff and our rounds have shown that classroom management is an impediment to student success, our instructional team may identify one of a list of strong starts to class (meeting students at the door, having a structured process for entering the classroom, working with materials, and having engaging independent activities for students upon arrival) to select as a schoolwide practice to measure impact.

This became a great evaluation of questions asked that noted the evidence that was being offered as a pattern. These patterns of practice that are generated as a result of our learning walks then become the focus of our analysis of student work, so let's move to the analysis phase.

How the Process Works Together

The process is where you learn. The process is where you grow. The process is where you develop character and find out who you are. It's the only path to your goals. The process is the point. — Matt Hogan

Here is an example of how this process can work together in collaboration with your other school teams. You probably already have teams or committees in your building that engage in work that is designed to support student achievement and improvement and to look at the needs of teachers to grow capacity. What I like about the rotation of data, planning, learning, rounds, analysis of student work, and mini-clinics is it takes the already existing structure of professional learning communities and organizes it in a logical sequence that can then transfer to school improvement, professional development, multi-tiered systems, and other support structures. This is where the true power lies. Using this overarching framework allows evidence from multiple different sources to come together and align.

For example, a school improvement action we identified to increase instructional rigor in our math classes was to improve student discourse. The first round of learning walks that we conducted as a team was with the sole purpose of determining whether any student discourse was occurring in math classrooms. We simply tallied whether students were offered opportunities to discuss content during their math class, and if they were offered an opportunity, the team recorded the question that was asked. The instructional team reviewed the results and recognized that while students were given the task to turn and talk during most of their math classes, the questions we wrote down were not questions of substance that provided students with the opportunity to engage in mathematical discourse and deep thinking about mathematical concepts. Generally, the questions simply asked students to discuss the answers they got on a particular math problem.

> ...at the beginning of the year, the learning rounds that the instructional team conducts are to "see what we see" based on our communicated expectations, vision, and school improvement actions.

This initial investigation informed our focus for further examination of practice by teachers. The teachers conducted the next round of learning walks with the expressed intent to examine and collect data around the level of questions asked by teachers and the resulting impact on students' mathematical understanding. This process was critical to our teachers recognizing that our students were not gaining foundational mathematical understanding due to the limited opportunities to engage in meaningful discourse and the limited number of questions that prompted higher-level thinking in students.

The opportunity for teachers to see for themselves that there was a gap in what we thought we were building in student understanding and the actual practice that was occurring in our classrooms became a foundational cultural shift that moved teacher practice. The information was taken to our school improvement team, and the resulting action included the addition of student dialogue prompts in our lesson plans, the collection of exit tickets that showed an increased understanding of mathematical concepts, and increased reflective practice as evidenced by our planning PLCs.

CHAPTER 6

Conclusion

Experience is the only thing that brings knowledge, and the longer you are on Earth, the more experience you are sure to get.   -The Wizard of Oz

There is a myth of sorts in the medical community. In the US, it is referred to as the July Effect. In the UK, it is called the Killing Season. These two terms refer to the time of year when new physicians traditionally begin their residency training. This complex and perhaps over-sensationalized time earned the term because of the thought that newly minted physicians make more mistakes than a seasoned doctor when it comes to patient care. It is the learning and doing curve of the medical field. A 2017 study in the Journal of the American

Medical Association (JAMA) found that teaching hospitals have lower mortality rates than nonteaching hospitals (Burke, et.al.). Hospitals that have strong teaching and learning experiences through a rounds process that when the process of that round is structured and supervised by strong physicians and doctors are not only learning the right things but given the opportunity to see excellent patient care and provide patient care under supervision can reassure the public that time of year should not be a concern for adequate care.

To ease your mind, there is no strong conclusive evidence to support the idea of the July Effect, but it has not stopped the medical field from instituting strong practices of learning rounds, particularly in hospitals designated as teaching hospitals. After my experiences observing a strong teaching hospital's care for my mother, I am convinced that a similar practice of strong learning rounds for educators holds significant promise for developing strong and effective practices for all teachers. In this time when the teaching population is diminishing and those entering the teaching profession have not all followed the traditional path through teacher education programs, we must consider providing job-embedded experiences such as those the learning rounds approach highlight.

The process of learning rounds has brought about change that I don't believe would have been possible without a structure to support such work. While the processes explained in this book may include familiar individual activities when it comes to school improvement, putting it all together into a logical workflow helped my schools build a reflective practice and increase student achievement.

What I have learned about this process of school transformation through learning rounds and building reflective practices is the value of the capacity we already possess before we even begin to examine the work.

It reminds me of my move from elementary to middle school as a school leader. It was an emotional move to make as my staff and I had worked hard in the previous years to develop strong practices and to hold each other accountable for our teaching and learning. I knew I was going to miss this staff immensely, so the final staff meeting was very emotional. The staff knew that one of my favorite movies is The Wizard of Oz so they decorated our media center in true Oz fashion, complete with Dorothy's ruby red slippers in the center of the table.

When it came time to say my final parting words after food, fun, laughter, and a few tears, I stood before my staff and recalled the final scene in the movie, where Glenda the Good Witch appears before Dorothy. She responds to Dorothy's plea, "Oh, will you help me? Can you help me?" with, "You don't need to be helped any longer; you've always had the power." To this, the scarecrow asks, "Well, why didn't you tell her that before?" Glenda simply states, "Because she wouldn't have believed me. She had to experience it for herself."

This experience sums up what I believe to be the purpose and power of learning rounds with teachers – they already have the power of great teaching for an enormous impact on all students, but they can't simply be told this. They must experience it for themselves.

That is what learning rounds and building reflective practice does for transforming schools, and that is my wish for each and every leader and educator who uses this book as a jumping-off point to do so.

The following resources may be downloaded and printed for personal use at:

https://sites.google.com/view/leadlearners/home

LEARNING ROUNDS WITH TEACHERS • 83

RESOURCE 1

Focus Organizer
Using Capacity Walks to Improve Capacity

FAST FACTS: WHAT THE DATA SAYS

Math Proficiency: _____

ELA Proficiency: _____

Science Proficiency: _____

Social Studies Proficiency: _____

Other Subjects or Data: _____

Behavior: _____

Attendance: _____

OBSERVATION TRENDS

_____
_____
_____
_____
_____
_____
_____
_____
_____
_____

CIRCLE OR HIGHLIGHT THE TOP 3 CONCERNS

PRIORITY OF CHANGING THE CONCERN

USE 0, 1, OR 2 TO IDENTIFY THE LEVEL OF PRIORITY FOR EACH CONCERN. LEVEL 0 IS LOW PRIORITY CONCERN, LEVEL 2 IS HIGH CONCERN. CONSIDER THE LEVEL OF QUICK WIN, EASE OF TRANSFER, AND TIME NEEDED TO CHANGE THAT THE CONCERN INVOLVES.

	QUICK WIN	EASE OF TRANSFER	TIME NEEDED TO CHANGE
① _____	☐	☐	☐
② _____	☐	☐	☐
③ _____	☐	☐	☐

IDENTIFIED FOCUS

_____
_____
_____
_____
_____
_____
_____

RESOURCE 2

LEARNING WALKS CHECKLIST

Use this checklist to plan your team walkthroughs.

LOGISTICS ✓

Determine the focus of the instructional round.

Examine master schedule for best opportunities to observe your focus.

Use planning sheet to identify day, time, and classes.

Create a list of individuals that will conduct rounds and the time they have available.

Determine time and location for follow up if it will not occur immediately after leaving a classroom.

Secure "Thank You's" for visiting classrooms.

Schedule follow up administrative or professional development meeting to discuss next steps.

RESOURCE 3

Name: _____ Date: _____

Noticings

What is the Teacher Doing/Saying	What are the students Doing/Saying

RESOURCE 4

NAME: _____   DATE: _____

SCHEDULE
Focus: _____

Guiding Questions

1. What is the purpose of the lesson?
2. What evidence exists to show this was the right lesson for students?
3. What are students doing to demonstrate the thinking?
4. How are students supported in their thinking?

Time	Teacher	Subject
_____	_____	_____
_____	_____	_____
_____	_____	_____
_____	_____	_____
_____	_____	_____
_____	_____	_____
_____	_____	_____
_____	_____	_____
_____	_____	_____
_____	_____	_____
_____	_____	_____
_____	_____	_____
_____	_____	_____
_____	_____	_____

RESOURCE 5

NAME: _____ DATE: _____

NOTES

Focus: _____

Guiding Questions

- WHAT IS THE TASK?
- WHAT IS THE STANDARD ALIGNED TO THE TASK?
- WHAT BEST PRACTICES DID THE TEACHER EMPLOY?
- WHAT IS THE EVIDENCE OF STUDENT LEARNING BASED ON TEACHER ACTIONS?

Student Arrangement

RESOURCE 6

LEARNING ROUNDS SCHEDULE

Please meet at the assigned teacher's classroom door at the time designated.

Learning Round Participant	Time	Teacher & Room #

Guiding Questions

What is the purpose of the lesson?

What evidence exists to show this was the right lesson for students?

What are students doing that demonstrate their thinking?

How are students supported in their thinking?

RESOURCE 7

Guiding Questions Record Sheet

Teacher _____

WHAT IS THE LEARNING TARGET?
_____
_____

WHAT EVIDENCE SHOWS THE STUDENTS ARE AWARE OF THE LEARNING TARGET?
_____
_____
_____
_____

HOW DOES THE WORK OF STUDENTS ALIGN TO THE LEARNING STANDARD?
_____
_____
_____
_____

HOW WILL THE TEACHER KNOW WHEN THE LEARNING TARGET IS MET?
_____
_____
_____
_____
_____

RESOURCE 8

Analysis of Student Work

Teacher _____. Date _____

TARGET(S)

Standard(s): _____
Intended
Outcome(s): _____
_____
_____

STUDENT DATA CHART

LACKING UNDERSTANDING	APPROACHING UNDERSTANDING	FULL UNDERSTANDING
# OF STUDENTS ___	# OF STUDENTS ___	# OF STUDENTS ___
% OF STUDENTS ___	% OF STUDENTS ___	% OF STUDENTS ___
WHAT CAN STUDENTS:	**WHAT CAN STUDENTS:**	**WHAT CAN STUDENTS:**
DO:	DO:	DO:
NOT DO:	NOT DO:	NOT DO:

WHAT NEXT?

SKILLS:	SKILLS:	SKILLS:
STRATEGIES:	STRATEGIES:	STRATEGIES:
REASSES:	REASSES:	REASSES:
LACKING	APPROACHING	FULL

References

Ambrose, S. A., Bridges, M. W., DiPietro, M., Lovett, M. C., & Norman, M. K. (2010). How Learning Works: Seven Research-Based Principles for Smart Teaching.

Burke L.G., Frakt, A.B., Khuller, D., Orav, E., Jha, A., (2017). Association between teaching status and mortality in US hospitals. JAMA 317(20), 2105-2113.

City, E.A., Elmore, R.F., Fiarman, S.E, &Teitel, L. (2009) Instructional Rounds in Education: A network approach to improving teaching and learning. Cambridge, Massachusetts: Harvard Education Press.

Fisher, D., & Frey, N. (2014). Using teacher learning walks to improve instruction. Principal Leadership, 14(5), 58-61.

Hattie, J., & Zierer, K. (2017). 10 Mindframes for visible learning: Teaching for success. Routledge.

Lezotte, L. W. (1991). Correlates of effective schools: The first and second generation.

Philpott, Carey and Oates, C. (2015) Learning Rounds: What the literature tells us (and what it doesn't), Scottish Educational Review 47(1), 49-65.

Pink, DH. When: The Scientific Secrets of Perfect Timing. New York: Riverhead Books; 2018.

Stoll , L., Bolam, R., McMahon, A., Wallace, M. & Thomas, S. (2006) Professional learning communities: A review of the literature, Journal of Educational Change, 7, 221-25.

About the Author

Marcy is a veteran educator who has spent most of her career as a coach of teachers and school leaders. Her experiences at the classroom, school, district, and state levels provide a unique perspective for educators looking to transform schools and drive student achievement. Dr. Roan is an accomplished school leader with proven results at the elementary and middle school levels in both Title 1 and non-Title 1 schools. This book helps new and veteran school leaders establish and support the learning rounds process with teachers and instructional coaches to develop a culture of reflective practice and collaborative efficacy. This book is designed to drive school improvement and student achievement by using the collaborative learning approach thought to be exclusively for the medical profession.

Photography by Kelli Gowdy
http://kelligowdyphotography.com

Made in the USA
Las Vegas, NV
21 August 2023